J
636.8
PET

BrT

3.54

DOLTON PUBLIC LIBRARY DISTRICT

3 1146 00207 2605

D1418488

FIRST PETS

Cats

Kate Petty

BARRON'S

DOLTON PUBLIC LIBRARY DIST.
849-2385

Hunter and pet

Cats belong to the same family as lions and tigers.
Watch a cat stalking a bird and you can see that
it is a silent hunter like its larger cousins.
Even well fed pets will still hunt for sport.
Cats always hunt alone but they like to be
with people too. They have been kept as pets for
thousands of years. Cats often live for 15 years.

A Silver Spotted Tabby stalking.

A tiny fly won't make a meal but it's good hunting practice for this Tabby kitten. ▷

207-2605

Dolton Public Library District

3

All kinds of cats

What sort of cat would you choose? A fluffy Persian, a smooth Abyssinian or a chocolate-and-cream Siamese with unusual blue eyes? There are about 30 types of pedigree cats. Even non-pedigree cats come in lots of different colors – white or black or ginger, often a mixture of all three. Tabby cats can have very beautiful markings too.

Long-haired Persian

Ruddy Abyssinian

This Siamese kitten has pale blue eyes and a loud meow. ▷

Good-looking cats

Soft fur, large eyes and long whiskers make a cat pretty to look at. But all these things help it to be a good hunter, too. A furry cat moves silently on soft paws. Its large eyes adapt quickly to darkness or bright lights. A cat's whiskers are as long as the widest part of its body – if the whiskers go through a hole then the rest of the body can follow.

A Tortoiseshell British Shorthair washes its fur and whiskers.

A cat's pupils are narrow in daylight. After dark they become wider to let in more light. ▷

Graceful movers

Most cats move quickly and smoothly.
They can curl up tightly or stretch out
because their skeletons are so flexible.
From a low, crouching position a cat can leap
onto a high wall or from one branch to another.
A cat nearly always makes a perfect landing,
even when it jumps from a great height.

American Blue-cream Shorthair showing its sharp claws.

Tabby cat leaping from a tall tree to land gently. ▷

Eating

Wild cats eat their kill and then sleep for hours. Even tiny kittens can seem quite wild when they eat, sometimes growling fiercely to make sure no one steals their food. Cats eat mainly meat and always need water to drink. They enjoy fish and milk too. It is good for them to eat grass sometimes.

Red Mackerel Tabby Persian crouching over its food.

Cats will always choose a favorite place for curling up to sleep. ▷

Angry cats

You can always tell when a cat is angry. A waving tail and flattened ears are warning signs. When a cat arches its back and makes its fur stick out, it is usually trying to scare off another cat or a dog. Have you ever heard cats fighting? They hiss and yowl as they circle around each other, waiting for the moment to lash out with their claws.

The Red Burmese cat backs off from the Black one.

At only thirteen weeks old this Tabby kitten bravely displays its anger. ▷

The independent cat

Some cats love to be stroked and petted at any time, but others will be affectionate only when it suits them.
Most cats will come when they are called at mealtimes, but usually they come and go as they please.
Cats like to find out things for themselves. They are always curious about a dripping faucet or an open box. Sometimes their curiosity leads them into mischief.

This Blue Abyssinian obviously enjoys being stroked.

It's time for this curious Tabby to go and play somewhere else! ▷

Newborn kittens

A mother cat is pregnant for nine weeks.
She looks for a quiet place to have her kittens.
There are usually three or four kittens in a litter.
Their ears are tiny and their eyes are tightly shut.
They drink milk from their mother and sleep
curled up against her. If the kittens are disturbed
too often, the mother will carry them in her mouth
to a more quiet place.

A Tortoiseshell and White British Shorthair feeding her kittens.

A mother cat carries the kitten by the scruff of its neck. ▷

Growing up

Kittens open their eyes about ten days after birth.
Soon they can stagger to their feet. Small kittens,
with their soft fur and stubby tails, are adorable, but
they must be treated like babies, not like toys.
At six to eight weeks they can eat solid food
and drink from a saucer. Now they are old
enough to leave home.

**A Tabby kitten at play
is practicing to be a hunter.**

Kittens play fighting their first battles against their brothers and sisters. ▷

Handle with care

You should always be careful when handling a cat. If it doesn't want to be held it might scratch you. Always treat a cat with respect and remember that it has a mind of its own. Approach it gently and hold it comfortably. Support the cat underneath and hold it firmly around the chest.

This kitten is well supported and secure.

A cat will usually warn you if it wants you to stay away. ▷

Know your cats

This chart will help you to recognize some of the different breeds of cats. A cat show is the best place to see them all.
Cats vary in shape, type of hair and color.
Different cats also have different natures.
A Persian cat hates to be teased but the Rex loves to play games. A Siamese can be noisy but the Abyssinian is usually quiet.

Siamese

Burmese

Angora

Rex

Abyssinian

Tabby

Persian
Chinchilla

Colorpoint

British Shorthair

Persian

23

Index

Photographic credits:

Cover: Zefa; pages 3, 5, 7, 9, 13 and 15: Bruce Coleman; page 11: Greg Evans; pages 17 and 21: Spectrum; page 19: Sally Anne Thompson/ Animal Photography.

Design   David West Children's
                    Book Design
Illustrations   George Thompson
Picture Research Cee Weston-Baker

First paperback edition for the United States and Canada published 1993 by Barron's Educational Series, Inc.

First published in the United States 1989 by Gloucester Press.

© Aladdin Books Ltd 1989

All rights reserved.

All inquiries should be addressed to:
Barron's Educational Series, Inc.
250 Wireless Boulevard
Hauppauge, NY 11788

Library of Congress
Catalog Card No. 88-83087
International Standard
Book No. 0-8120-1485-5 (paperback)

Library of Congress Cataloging-in-Publication Data

Petty, Kate
    Cats/ Kate Petty:
    illustrations, George Thompson.
    24 p : col. ill : 23 cm - (First pets)

    Includes index.
    ISBN 0-8120-1485-5 (paperback)

1. Cats-Juvenile literature. I. Thompson, George, 1944 -ill.
II. Title. III. Series: Petty, Kate. First Pets

SF445.7.P375 1989   88-83087
                          AACR 2 MARC

PRINTED IN BELGIUM

3456   98765432